COSBY

TENN.
N.C.

40

NAL PARK

CATALOOCHEE

ASHEVILLE →

RIVER

MAGGIE
VALLEY

19

23
74

OCONALUFTEE
FARMSTEAD

WAYNESVILLE

MOUNT PISGAH
(SLIDING ROCK) →

EROKEE

SYLVA

ILLSBORO

BLUE RIDGE PARKWAY

N
W ⊕ E
S

441
23

FRANKLIN,
HIGHLANDS,
TALLULAH GORGE
↓

MOUNTAINS
In The Mist

Also by Roger Bansemer

The Art of Hot-Air Ballooning
Southern Shores
Rachael's Splendifilous Adventure
At Water's Edge

For my daughters
Lauren and Rachael

Calligraphy by Linda Renc

Thanks to:
Jean Duncan
Tom Robbins

Published by Taylor Publishing Company
1550 West Mockingbird Lane
Dallas, Texas 75235

Library of Congress Cataloging-in-Publication Data

Bansemer, Roger.
    Mountains in the mist : the Great Smokies / Roger Bansemer.
        p.   cm.
    ISBN 0-87833-839-X
    1. Great Smoky Mountains (N.C. and Tenn.)—Pictorial works.   2. Mountan
life—Great Smoky Mountains (N.C. and Tenn.)—Pictorial works.   3. Natural
history-Great Smoky Mountains (N.C. and Tenn.)—Pictorial works.   I. Title.
F443,G7B36 1993   93-19261
976.8'89—dc20   CIP

Printed in the United States of America
10 9 8 7 6 5 4

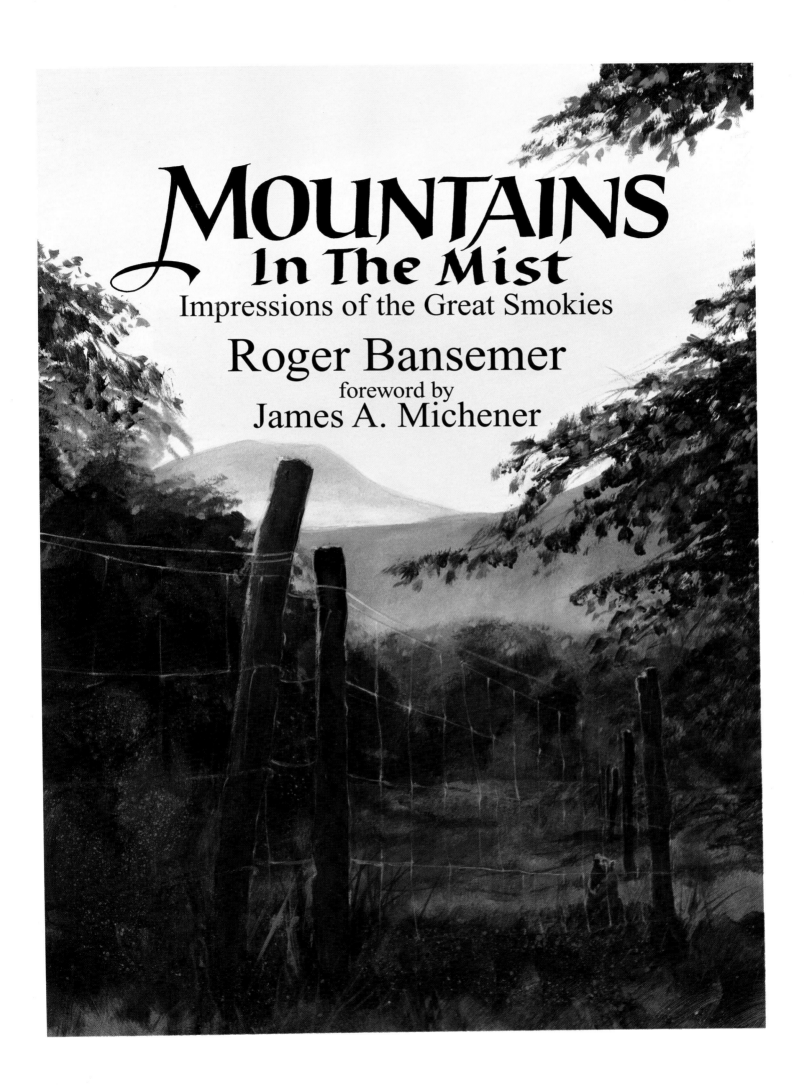

MOUNTAINS
In The Mist
Impressions of the Great Smokies

Roger Bansemer

foreword by
James A. Michener

Foreword

A friend owed me a debt which could not properly be discharged with money, so, in a burst of genius, he gave me a copy of *Southern Shores* by Roger Bansemer, an artist-naturalist from nearby Clearwater. It was a handsome affair, beautiful color plates of the rich wildlife that exists along the unique shorelines of Florida. Here were the pelicans, the egrets, the great blue herons, the *Washingtonia* palms, never seen in the north, and all the features that make towns like Tampa and St. Petersburg so rich in natural beauty.

What my friend who gave it could not have known was that his gift arrived just as I was in the process of drawing my own portraits of the very birds and trees and shrubs depicted in the Bansemer book. I was doing this because I had in the back of my mind the idea that I might want to write, one of these days, a book about some aspect of life in semitropical Florida, and here was a major part of my research already done for me, in fine style and in full color. *Southern Shores* was a godsend, the best gift I'd received in years.

In fact, I was so favorably impressed by it that I sat immediately down and typed out a fan letter to the author, praising him for the excellent work he'd done and inviting him to stop by where I was living not far from his home, and like all the writers I know, he jumped at the chance of a free meal. After lunch we walked through the woods near my home and he explained aspects of the wild life that had captivated me so powerfully. Under his tutelage I saw things that I had not noticed closely before, and a friendship developed, because I realized that with his artist's eye he could see things I didn't.

After several meetings, an amazing coincidence surfaced. He was deep in the process of painting and writing his next book, an account of living habitats in the colorful mountain country that includes western North Carolina and eastern Tennessee, forming The Great Smoky Mountains National Park. When I visited his studio I found that he had completed about ninety per cent of his illustrations and a fair portion of the text to accompany them. The proposed book promised to be just as engaging as his *Southern Shores.*

What he could not know was that for some time I had become increasingly involved with a novel I might want to write about aspects of life in western Florida, the scene of *Southern Shores,* and the mountains of Tennessee-North Carolina, the locale of *Mountains in the Mist*, the title of his new book. Thus we were engaged in identical research problems, although with vastly different end results in mind.

He spoke first: "You said the other day that you knew the Highlands district of North Carolina rather well. That could be judged as an extension of the area I'm focusing on. Since you liked my last book would you consider doing the foreword to my book, when it's finished?"

A writer like me receives many such requests, most of them irrelevant, because an ordinary foreword does little to help the sales of a book. That's especially true when the writer in question has no serious affiliation with the subject matter of the book. The few forewords I've done have amounted to little, but I concede that if James Baldwin, the fine black writer, had said of a beginning black novelist, "This is a splendid work by a young man who knows what he's writing about," such an endorsement might be significant. Mine aren't.

So I was inclined to say "No!" to Bansemer's suggestion, except that our mutual work plans coincided so beautifully that to comply was most tempting: "If you can leave tomorrow for an expedition to the Great Smoky Mountains National Park, so that I can see what you're trying to do and whether it's real or not, it's a deal. You drive. I'll pay for the gas."

Next night, at ten o'clock, he
met me after the close of the seminar on
creative writing I was conducting in a small Florida college,
and we set off for an all-night drive north to the mountains. Our round trip
would cover 1485 miles of exciting countryside.   We slept in the rear of his
spacious van, ate at drive-ins, and explored in deep detail not only the mountains and valleys but also the scenes of daily living that Roger had illustrated
in his paintings. And gradually, after having visited a score of settings with
which I was already familiar from his
paintings, I began to appreciate
the ambitious task he had set
for himself.

By painting in acrylics and
describing in words the buildings and
procedures of the past century, he was
endeavoring to perpetuate the colorful
ways of mountain life. But he was *not* dealing
sentimentally with eye-catching relics of the past; he
was concentrating on buildings which were currently
occupied, on people who were right now preserving many
of the old ways. Often as we visited some scene he had
caught perfectly in his art and words, I thought: "It's
lucky he came along when he did and took the
pains he did. Because ten years
from now this record might
be lost."

What I saw as we probed various crannies tucked away in the hills of Tennessee and North Carolina was the past clinging to the last vestiges of life in the present. It was a compelling experience which, I believe, Bansemer has captured in this book.

While travelling, we met the quintessential mountain man, a real fellow who tracked us down when we were parked at Tallulah Gorge, studying the chasm across which the famous acrobat Karl Wallenda walked on a tightrope in 1970. The congenial figure who stepped forward to greet us could not have known we were coming to that spot, or that we were even in the vicinity. He was, like all the people Roger painted, a very real man.

In Habersham County, I found a spot of peculiar interest to me. For many years I had served on a committee of our Postal Service and am currently engaged in the construction of a major historical museum depicting the history of our postal customs.

From here, in this small, remote village, came Joseph Habersham, who served as postmaster general for three presidents: Washington, Adams, and Jefferson. He was largely responsible for getting our national postal service extended and properly based.

At the Pioneer Farmstead near the eastern edge of the Park, I was enchanted by the manner in which old farm buildings had been preserved along the banks of a flowing stream. They recapitulated a wealth of family history, for it was in such buildings that our pioneer families toiled to build the nation.

I enjoyed the care with which Bansemer created his images of the pig and explained in his text the importance of this humble animal during the years of our westward expansion.

It was fun seeing the incredible jumble of Popcorn Sutton's junkyard posing as a center for antiques, but my more lasting impressions came from the old buildings depicted in Bansemer's paintings: old barns, the tub mill, a contraption that was unfamiliar to me, the various country stores, and especially the old houses in which the mountain people had lived in times past or were occupying even today.

Great Smoky Mountains National Park is well regarded not only for its colorful landscapes and restful valleys, but also for the people who have through the centuries wrestled a hard, meager living from its soil. Bansemer catches the faces of these people, and they provide the human coloring to this book.

In retrospect, I'm glad Roger invited me to write this foreword, because the study involved enabled me to inspect in close detail a corner of our republic about which I would myself be writing. And what I saw assured me that he had produced a fine book. I hope it does well.

And what of my own project? As I wandered these mountain paths and relished their grand vistas I found myself in quandary. When I was in Tennessee, I said: "This is exactly what I've been seeking! But when I crossed over into North Carolina I found it equally rewarding and cried with vigor: "This has got to be it! I can see it now!" Soon I shall have to choose between them.

James A. Michener

There are certain places on earth that are special in a way that's difficult to define. It is usually a particular place like the house we grew up in, something that has specific memories attached to it, but sometimes it encompasses a whole area.

The Smoky Mountains are special to me and have been for many years. As a boy on vacation with my parents, I can remember sitting in the back of the car looking out the window. A scene like this quickly passed by my view and I anxiously waited for the vista around the next bend in the road.

I don't know exactly what touches me about these mountains. It's a feeling more than anything, I suppose. In any case, the Smoky Mountains must certainly touch others like they touch me. More than nine million visitors come here each year for the same reasons I do.

Abandoned and almost forgotten. You know when a chimney starts to fall down, the house isn't far behind in sharing the same fate. Chimneys are usually the last to go. I wonder how many lives have passed through this house. How many happy moments and sad ones these walls could recall. All returning to the land now. Being swallowed up by Old Father Time and new summer foliage.

One reason people like to visit the Smokies is the diversity they offer, something which everyday life seems to lack. The infinite variation of textures can be found everywhere you look.

Visiting the mountains renews my appreciation for what time creates. Too often we are led to believe that for something to be good, it has to be new, yet the elements and harsh conditions that the years deliver bring a wonderful distinctiveness and sense of unity to this area of the world.

Eastern Fence Lizard

Salamanders are very secretive creatures and live under rocks for the most part. They are more prevalent than lizards in the mountains. They like seldom-used places, such as this near the woods, where they can get out in the sunshine to warm up.

The eastern fence lizard is fast but will freeze when he sees you, hoping that you didn't see him. Although they look threatening, they aren't harmful and don't mind being held once you catch them. If you rub their heads, they'll stay with you for quite a while.

Red Salamander

Five-lined Skink

Tallulah Falls Gorge

This is probably my all-time favorite stop along the route to the Smokies when I drive up from Florida. As a small boy I remember my parents stopping here for a break and now I do the same with my daughters. It was once on the main drag of route 441, but now a bypass can quickly take you past this wonderful spot, unless you are watching for it.

The great tight-rope walker Karl Wallenda walked across this gorge back in July of 1970, and some posters of the event once graced the nearby souvenir stand. I don't know how long the gift shop will remain now that it has been cut off from the main highway, but the view of the gorge will always remain there for a memorable rest stop.

Not far from the overlook, lies a concrete and metal structure. It was built to anchor Wallenda's tight-rope.

This is the man James Michener and I met at Tallulah Gorge. He had the kind of face artists like me enjoy painting and his character was in keeping with the look he portrayed. After talking awhile, he rummaged through debris on the floor of his pickup truck and found a homemade tape of original songs proudly sung and accompanied on guitar by himself. He invited us to listen and we did with interest. They were pretty good. The music persevered but I didn't. I excused myself to attend to soup I had heating in the van, leaving Michener to find his own way out.

It was a brief but fascinating chance meeting. He went on his way and so did we.

During one of my visits to the Smokies, I stopped for the night at Hot Springs, North Carolina. It is one of those quiet little towns where nothing ever happens. That evening I ate at a small restaurant where I was the only customer at the time. Later my white German shepherd and I walked down the quiet streets looking at the sights and enjoying the cool air. Just perfect.

This is a view of the French Broad River just outside Hot Springs.
Late afternoon, when the last flow of light filters over the mountains.
I sat there for a long time, quiet, just watching the light fade.

Luna moths start to appear. The moonlike
circles on its wings help to fool birds into
thinking they are the eyes of a larger animal.

Fireflies show up as darkness falls. These wonders of
nature continue to fascinate me as they did when
I was a boy. The light they give off produces no heat
and its flashing is used to attract mates. I've always
called them lightning bugs.

On another afternoon as I was exploring
a little-traveled back road, I saw this man with
his dog and decided to stop and talk to him,
a total stranger. I told him that I was from
Florida and we started a conversation.
He said he had visited Florida back in
1941 just before the war, but this was
his home and the home of his father.
The house had been in the family
over 100 years. He had lived in this
house all his life. I got the impression
that he had not wandered very far
from here for the most part of his life.
Everyone knew him around these
parts, he told me with great satisfaction.

Houses sometimes acquire a character where windows begin to look strangely like eyes and a nose-shaped chimney breathes smoke. Although vague, it all seems to fit together to give this dwelling and others like it a sort of human quality.

Some of these homesteads which have stood gracefully against time for more than a century are not without nearby contrasting improvements of space age technology. It's a strange and unexpected contrast between necessities and luxuries. The house goes without paint and attention like some forgotten friend while the inhabitants sit inside and stare at satellite television beamed in from outer space.

I've found that most people in the Smokies are quite friendly
when a stranger like me strays up to their home.

When I ask if I can make some sketches of their house
for a book I'm working on, their first response is, "What on earth would you want to draw
an old place like this for?" Then they seem pleased when they realize that someone else
appreciates that which means so much to them.

Inside, these houses are filled with their memories and stories. Faded pictures
from the past crowd every mantle and each fractured wooden table that has seen years
of use is covered with the tarnished metal frames of rigid ancestors posed like mannequins.
The buildings are typically not well kept, but they do represent significantly deep roots
for most of the people who live inside.

I'm envious of people who have these little "out buildings." It seems I'm always running out of room to put things.

I have mixed feelings about old tires that are made into flower pots. I admire them as long as they're not in my yard. I find the notion of transforming a worn-out tire into a useful item appealing.

The simple and basic shape of a home expresses to me a belief in what is fundamental. Importance rooted in principles and not in decoration. Most new homes totally lack the charm and beauty that this spartan structure of unpretentious materials has. Artists have always focused in on it, but decorators and architects have lost this sense of simplicity.

To make the architecture of any mountain home complete, you need the accessories of a couple skinny hound dogs.

It would never occur to me to have a red roof on a house, but in this case someone had the imagination and taste to pull it off. I've driven past this place many times and it has always caught my attention and interest.

Spring houses still exist around some of the old homesteads. Most are in a state of disrepair and, given another generation or so, they will have all disappeared

I can remember my mom using one of these machines.
Clothes would always get jammed up in those yellowish-colored
wringers. Sometimes water would go all over the floor.

This is where tales about the past were handed down from generation to generation, or where the family sat lazily after enjoying that biggest meal of the week, Sunday dinner. Since this country began, the porch has been <u>the</u> place to discuss politics and the world situation, or swap gossip with neighbors about the town and its people.

Today most homes don't even have a front porch. Television and air conditioning have taken its place and the front porch swing hangs silently as an icon to past memories.

When I see a plow used to support a mailbox, it reminds me that an era has passed. It represents a time when most of our population lived in a rural setting. A period when agriculture depended entirely on animal power and hard manual labor. It represents a part of this country's history that fewer and fewer people can remember and more people have difficulty relating to.

After a few years of use,
mailboxes start to take on a weather-worn
personality of their own, like old and familiar
faces. We take them for granted but would quickly
miss them if they disappeared. They're our quiet connection
to family and friends. Even "bulk rate" mail can often greet us
with a few moments away from a busy day.

I have done a small amount of stone work, enough to appreciate the incredible skill and patience it takes to master the discipline. There are so many skills such as this that go unnoticed until you personally give them a try, then you get a genuine understanding of the ability to even partially succeed in accomplishing such a job.

This particular stone work was on the summer home of Joseph Habersham (1751-1815). ↓

He was a patriot, an active political leader, served as a colonel in the Revolutionary War and as postmaster general under Presidents Washington, Adams, and Jefferson.

Habersham County remembers Joseph Habersham with a nearby bronze plaque telling curious passersby his story. Yet I wonder how much more important in the eyes of God are his accomplishments for whom the county was named than the legacy of that nameless craftsman who put together this flawless stone work which still stands today as a monument to his labors. I think they are pretty much equal in standing.

Churches of this area have kept to a simplicity of shape. They represent the strong and unshakable beliefs of the people who years ago settled here. The building in itself is a statement of strength.

The surrounding mountains are also cathedrals of unequaled majesty. The sight of a white spire only adds as a reminder of God's wonders.

A nearby house, where the pastor might live, echoes the basics of the church building.

Where we live may be one of the
larger choices or accidents that life
brings our way. It may be on a hill
or we might find ourselves in the valley.
I wonder how the differences really
affect our outlook on life.

Queen Anne's lace blooms throughout the summer just
about everywhere in the Smoky Mountains. Each plant
has about 500 individual flowers, with a single
deep red or purple flower in the center of each of the
smaller clusters.

The flower got its name, according to one folk tale,
from the red flower symbolizing a drop of blood caused
when Queen Anne (1665-1714) pricked her finger
while making lace.

It's also called wild carrot because it is closely
related. If you pull one up by the root you will
see why.

Clover can also be found just about anywhere,
especially along sunny roadsides and pastures.
The bumblebee is the only insect that can pollinate
clover with any success, so they are usually nearby.

This farmstead at the entrance to the Great Smoky Mountains National Park near Cherokee made an impression on me as a small boy that has lasted since visiting here with my parents years ago. It hasn't changed at all that I can tell and now I am showing my own children the same buildings that my parents so patiently brought me to see.

The cabin was built in 1901 by John E. Davis. His young sons, only four and eight years old at the time, hauled rocks for the chimney from the nearby river using a sled and oxen. Somehow I can't visualize my children doing anything like that!

My girls were dedicated to playing and running from building to building, and were not very interested in what these buildings represent. I was the same way when my parents brought me here. But one thing is for certain, the impressions it makes on them will also last a lifetime.

The Pioneer Farmstead as it is called is actually not "pioneer" at all. At the time these farm buildings were constructed, the pioneer period had long since ended. The word "pioneer" is often overused and misused.

Pioneers are usually thought of as the first permanent European settlers, who came to the Smokies during the late 1700's and early 1800's. The first European explorers, mainly Spanish, toured southern Appalachia long before that, in the 1500's.

However, it is important to remember that the Native American Indians were the true pioneers. They had been here hundreds of years before the first European ever set foot in these mountains.

Bees provided honey, as sugar was hard to
come by in early days. Hives were often made
from hollow logs, usually black gum trees.
It has a tendency to rot quickly on the inside
yet remain very hard on the outer edges,
ideal for a hollow hive. Notches were cut
at the bottom as an entrance for the bees.
Slats of wood would be placed inside and the
honey would be removed from these top layers
leaving the bottom of the hive undisturbed.
    The hollow logs were also used as storage
bins for cornmeal and flour.

    Down feathers used to fill pillows were the main
reason geese were raised, rather than as a food source.

An outhouse like this was a typical sight on many farms, although it was not unusual for many houses of the time to have no outhouse at all.

Corn was the single most important crop on the farm. It was roasted, ground into meal, and used in preparing many dishes, especially bread. Mats and mops were made from the shucks or they could be braided into rope and woven into dolls, hats and chair bottoms. Mattresses were stuffed with it. Pipes and tool handles were made from the cobs. And of course there was moonshine. Nothing went to waste.

The corn crib is where the corn was stored to dry. Loosely spaced logs aided in the circulation of air and prevented the corn from rotting. This crib was constructed so a wagon could drive underneath and the corn tossed over the log wall inside. The extra shelter area was for the storage of harnesses and tools and to keep a wagon out of the weather.

Even though many settlers disliked snakes and had superstitions about them, farmers would sometimes catch a black snake or two and place it in the corn crib to help keep mice away.

The barn was considered the headquarters of the farm. Built in the mid 1800's with no power tools and only simple axes and saws available, you can imagine what a job it was to construct a barn like this, with its large hand-hewn logs making up the stalls to the 16,000 shingles split from red oak.

This hay rake is also on the National Park Farmstead near Cherokee. Although it adds a nice touch to the scene, hay was not a common crop during the late 1800's and probably wouldn't have been on a farmstead like this. According to the 1897 census, only 7 of 45 families of the Oconaluftee District grew hay. It required hard work and many farms didn't bother since it was only used to feed livestock. The most common feed for animals was dried leaves from the corn stalk, called fodder.

Early farmers in the Smoky Mountains "would make do or do without" as the saying went, so the inventive spirit became a necessity. On this particular corn crib the roof was hinged, the wagon would pull along side, the roof propped open with a stick and the corn would be tossed in.

A small spring of cool water bubbles up from the rocks, down a wooden trough, through a spring house, and out the other side. This was the place to store milk, eggs, and butter, and also served as a source for the family's drinking water.

Evaporation of the water made the air inside cool and kept essentials inside from spoiling. If the spring house was large enough, buckets, tubs and other household items would be stored there. Sort of the same way things collect in closets at home.

It's also not a bad place to sit and cool off on a hot summer day.

Many early families hunted for food, but hunting was not always reliable. For that and other reasons pigs were raised on farms, and there were more of them than any other animal on the early mountain farm. An old saying goes, "You can use every part of the pig except the squeal." The portions of the pig that weren't eaten were put to other uses. If the intestines weren't eaten as chitlins, they were used as sausage casings. Lard was used for shortening, frying, and seasoning. Some inventive families even inflated the pig bladder to make balls for children to play with.

Pigs are basically clean animals, but they can't sweat, so about the only way they have to regulate their body temperature is to lie in the cool dirt or mud when it's hot. Extremely self-sufficient, they were allowed to forage the woods for themselves, eating many things that other livestock could not or would not eat, such as roots, berries, acorns, lizards and snakes. They don't make easy prey for predators either. It was unusual to find them in pens, except during the fall for fattening just before butchering. This pig is about five months old and can easily reach butchering size in less than a year.

The woodshed, always placed close to the house, was mainly for firewood. Hickory and oak were abundant, split relatively easily, and so were most commonly used. The ashes were ideal for producing lye, which in turn was used to make soap and as a cleaning agent. A weak solution is also part of the recipe for the making of hominy. Sometimes chicken coops would be attached to the back of a woodshed. The nearby chopping block used to split wood made a convenient place to sacrifice that evening's chicken dinner.

Having apple orchards was the sign of a prosperous farm and there were many among the Smoky Mountains. Apple houses like this were often built into the sides of hills to keep apples cool in summer. It also kept them from freezing in the winter. Being built of stone helped too. A small tunnel dug into a hill could also be used as an apple house.

This is park ranger and historian Tom Robbins. There are more than sixty such men and women in uniform who dedicate themselves to the Great Smoky Mountains National Park. They are always knowledgeable and kindhearted with help and information. Altogether there are 200 employees maintaining and keeping the park beautiful. They seldom get the credit they deserve.

This garden at the farmstead is representative of what a family would often grow. There was an emphasis to grow vegetables that were easy to preserve or that kept well through the winter. White and sweet potatoes, cabbage, turnips, onions and beans were grown.

The problem of bugs and weeds that gardeners deal with today was no less troublesome in the past. The difference is that families today don't have to depend on their gardens for food in the winter.

Many people saved seeds from year to year to plant again, though commercially available seeds have been around in this country for more than 200 years. Even before that, garden seed was imported from Europe. Peddlers also sold from door to door, especially in rural areas, until the introduction of mail order catalogs about 1830. That practice became even more popular in the late nineteenth and early twentieth centuries.

The Mason jar used to preserve food was patented in 1858, but it wasn't until later that home canning became popular. Many families preferred using more traditional methods like drying and pickling.

Of course, there is always a hungry critter willing to share what you have worked so hard to grow.

Gourds grow in a bizarre variety of shapes and sizes. Many were used as dippers and storage containers, but these birdhouse gourds are the ideal size and shape for the purple martin to nest in. They feed on insects and mosquitos while flying and seldom land on the ground, preferring a lofty perch for safety. They help keep the insect population to a minimum. That is why you always see martin houses near gardens.

"Apartments" with sometimes over 200 cubicles inside are often built just for these birds to nest in. About late July they head back to their winter homes in South America.

The martins return to the same site each spring.

Simple and
effective solutions to
problems have always fascinated
me, especially in this world of high-tech
gadgetry where everything gets complicated. Any
corporation faced with the problem of how to keep cows on one side of a fence
while still allowing easy passage for humans would certainly come up with some
mechanized gate involving droves of gears and moving parts. Here a simple
"V" shape prevents cattle from making the U-turn to the other side. It was
commonly called a "crazy gate."

Fences were an important part of any farm. They were designed to keep certain creatures from getting in and other creatures from getting out. Livestock was often allowed to roam and forage for itself. This made fences a necessity around gardens and crops.

Most of us call this a split rail fence. It was probably most common and certainly the type of fence that comes to mind when we think of fences in the Smoky Mountains, although there are many variations. This one is called a snake or worm fence. These fences were generally eight rails high. Sometimes ten. There was a saying about fences. They had to be "horse high, hog tight, and bull strong."

Some were cut from oak, but chestnut was preferred because of its availability and insect resistance. Chestnut was high in tannin, from which tannic acid for leather tanning was produced. This chemical made chestnut more resistant to insects, and a fence like this would last for many years.

This is called a post and rider fence.
Sometimes just one post was used and
the rails, after being stacked alternately
one upon another, were simply wired
to the pole to keep them from falling off.

Building a fence in this zig-zag configuration would take almost twice the amount of wood needed to build a fence in a straight line. With all the effort it took to cut and split trees into rails, you might wonder why they would build a fence in such a way. One reason is because they're moveable and were placed around haystacks or crops to keep animals out temporarily. Also, digging post holes is difficult or impossible in many areas because of the rocky ground.

Logs were split starting with a metal wedge or ax on one end. Then by using hardwood wedges - called gluts - placed along the length of the log, it would continue to be split by hitting the wedge with a maul. The maul was usually made from the trunk and root area of a hickory or white oak tree to give it strength and durability.

Black-eyed susans have always been a favorite of mine. They bloom in the summer, grow from one to two feet high with their fuzzy stems and leaves, and look especially lovely growing beside this fence.

dogwood glut with metal ring
(the ring was not always used)

maul

7-inch diameter hickory tree

iron wedge

No book on the Smokies would be complete without the black bear. Years ago they were a familiar sight while traveling through the park from Cherokee to Gatlinburg. You could always tell there was one alongside the road well before you actually saw it. Cars would be pulling over, traffic started to pile up and people were straining their necks at the upcoming sight. However, I have not seen a bear for years. Stricter rules about feeding, along with sturdy bear-proof trash containers, have discouraged frequent road-side panhandling from these creatures. They are no less plentiful though, just more apprehensive about showing themselves, since the days of picnic leftovers are less frequent.

The black bear has two or three cubs usually every other year. At birth, the cubs weigh only half a pound, about the size of a rat, and are blind, toothless, and practically hairless. Within two months, they have grown enough to venture outside the den.

They eat practically anything - berries, leaves, nuts, roots, insects, mice, chipmunks; they love fish and even enjoy digging into ant hills. They will let the ants crawl over their paws and then enthusiastically lick them off. Of course, we can't forget honey. Black bears eat the bees and all.

During the autumn, russet golds to cranberry reds begin to glaze the countryside in a glow of color. The leaves flutter from these tall sentries and fall to form a quilted carpet of color. If you listen, you can hear them. At times it occurs with a fury, as thermal drafts rush through the ridges. This cycle of enrichment draws thousands of visitors to view its splendor.

From this annual replenishment of organic fertility will come the premiere of spring, long after the leaves from deciduous trees have become part of the woodland floor.

No matter what weather conditions bring, the change of leaves is always a spectacle.

Trees need all the available water they have during the winter and leaves are shed for that reason. Fall colors are controlled by weather conditions, but there are many variables and even experts don't understand it all. Here are some factors that are known: The bright colors come from sugar stored in the leaves, and are improved by cool weather and sunshine. An early frost can reduce the colors by damaging leaves, contrary to what many think. Excessive rain, strong winds, and an early snow can also interfere with color changes.

As nature pours out its gift of colors, it also serves to camouflage the poisonous copperhead even more than usual among the leaves. I have never run into a copperhead or a rattlesnake in the mountains, but they do exist and it's a good idea to watch where you're stepping.

This is a beautiful time of the year. Rather than departing from the life of the summer into the dead of winter with a solemn face, the trees celebrate the transition with a fanfare of spectacular color.   What a wonderful lesson.

Ribbons of gravel wind through quiet and undisturbed forests.
I often set off on such roads not knowing where they may lead.

Early farmers often planted pumpkins in cornfields. They would keep well if protected from freezing and were used in winter as feed for livestock.

As winter comes to the mountains, food for deer becomes scarce. Having large appetites, eating more than a ton of food a year, they will eat just about anything in sight, from saplings and tree limbs to bushes from around the yard. Deer have even been known to gnaw the siding off of houses.

But aren't they beautiful creatures!

Smoke curling from stone and brick chimneys makes a vaporous exclamation mark
pointing to the human activity and warmth that dwells inside.
Outside everything is motionless and cold under the white carpet
of powder, frozen in time for the winter season.

When I visit the Smoky Mountains, my home base is with my friend, Bud Anderson, at his cabin. He once owned a fudge shop in Gatlinburg. I met him when I used to air-brush T-shirts there during the summer. He now lives on the Little Pigeon River not far from town.

I no longer paint shirts and he no longer makes fudge.

A gray sky makes the snow feel even colder.

Snow seems to fall in pockets here in the Smokies.
At times, one side of a mountain can be covered while
over the ridge remains untouched.

The harsh and clear-cut range of contrasts add to a sense of coldness during winter months as heavy moisture-filled clouds slowly drift between valleys. They generously add to the already frigid air.

Life can be so fragile yet so tenacious.
It's a wonder anything can survive in the
outdoors with the conditions that winter brings.

The snow crunches under the feet of cattle like the sound of
a new leather saddle as they walk in the snow. I wonder if they
suffer the cold to their hooves like we would on our feet?

On nearby fences, brittle stands of miniature ice sculptures
cover grassy clearings.

Spotlessly pressed shirts, still warm from the iron, were once delivered in this now rusted and forgotten shell.   All those shirts have long been turned into rags and the carriage that once made its daily rounds now sits silently, being absorbed back into the landscape from the harshness of the seasons.

Foot bridges are so inviting. If I spot one while driving, I usually interrupt my travels for a chance to walk on it.

I seldom explore where the bridge may lead, I'd rather sit for a few minutes and watch the leaves float by to their unknown destinations.

Two logs placed over a small stream with thick, rough-cut boards laid down on top make a simple and strong footbridge, sometimes called a corduroy bridge. Just the right kind of place to sit suspended with your thoughts over a silent stream, watch the world, and make a few quiet discoveries.

My girls, Lauren and Rachael, regard this as our all-time favorite swimming hole. It's a few miles from Gatlinburg on the Little Pigeon River at Greenbriar, part of the national park. I'll never understand how children can jump right into that freezing water!

Rachael would rather play on the warm rocks as Lauren unceasingly coaxes me into the Arctic-like water. "Come on dad, it's not cold." Sure! I always get in, but it takes a little while.

So many places to explore and things to do. I often wonder how simple childhood experiences like this might mold their lives.

That warm reflective glow on my children's faces will always be memorable to me. Nothing can compare to that.

Late afternoon arrives as a fine mist surrounds us.
The daylight begins to fade and so do we.

There is a magical attraction about waterfalls. Humans are compelled to
take notice of them. They can electrify our imagination with their never-ending
vitality. A few miles outside of Highlands, you will find several of the nicest
in the area, Bridal Veil Falls, which cascades 120 feet over the road, and
nearby Dry Falls.

Looking Glass Falls,
near Mt. Pisgah

Just up the road from
Looking Glass Falls, Sliding Rock
provides a natural playground for
children, young and old.

This looks like it could once have been a mill. Actually, it's a power plant built in 1927 and runs to this day, except for a few weeks in the fall when leaves tend to clog up the turbines. It generates enough electricity to serve 167 homes.

There are over forty species of fish within the Smoky Mountains National Park. This rainbow trout, along with the brown trout, are what most fly fishermen are hoping to catch.

I happened to see this mill out of the corner of my eye while traveling up 441. It was hidden back off the road. No signs pointed to it, no souvenir stand close by. Abandoned, just waiting for the wind and weather to take their final toll on the already weathered lumber, with only an occasional character hunter like me stumbling across it for a closer look.

This mill near Cherokee → is one of the most outstanding.

The mill at Pigeon Forge is still working after more than 160 years.

The construction of Fontana Dam
was started in 1942 and began to generate
electricity just three years later. Seven thousand
people worked on the project and at one point
5,500 people were working at one time.
The dam is 480 feet tall and the impressive
spillways are 34 feet in diameter.
The total cost was 70 million dollars.
According to records, $70,420,688.48 to be exact.
It was built primarily to supply electricity
to the Alcoa plant near Knoxville for the
making of aluminum during World War II
and helped energize Oak Ridge for efforts
to split the atom, which of course
at that time was secret.

Fontana Village is nearby. It was built to house workers temporarily while the dam was being constructed. Now it serves as a delightful resort.

This log house situated on the property was built in 1875 and is today a museum. It is one of the finest examples of dovetail craftsmanship anywhere in the Smokies and looking at it is a pleasure.

There is a tendency to call any structure built of logs a cabin, but a cabin was usually put together quickly and often for short-term use while a house was being built, so respectfully I call them log houses and the people living there years ago would have considered them such.

My parents and I vacationed here when I was eleven years old. The cabins haven't changed, and when I visited recently, it brought back many fond memories. One recollection was of tooling a leather belt with my dad in their craft shop. I still have that belt.

The rich organic breakdown of the many tree stumps, left from early timber-cutting generations ago, combined with seepage from underground springs creates micro-environments suiting a wealth of plants and mosses.

Sassafras

Daddy long-legs

Wooly bear

Maiden fern

Galax (round glossy leaf)

Lichen

florists sometimes use it.

Chestnut pod

Eastern box turtle

American Chestnut

Rhododendron seedling

Green stink-bug

Fan club-moss

Wild strawberries

Red maple

Here is a sample of what you can find under your feet on most any mountainside if you will only take a few moments to look.

Lichen

White-throated Sparrow

another stink-bug

Fungus

Mountain violets

Puff-balls (fungus)

Rattlesnake plantain

Black walnuts

Shining club-moss

Oak

Oak acorns

Sassafras leaf

The deciduous forests of the Smoky Mountains and surrounding areas create conditions conducive to supporting one of the broadest ranges of plant life in the world. Abundant rainfall, multidirectional exposures, varying soil types and altitudes, along with evolutionary changes account for this wealth and diversity of plant life. Only in parts of Asia and the Ozark Mountains in Arkansas do similar environments exist.

Unlike forests consisting primarily of evergreens, the deciduous hardwood forests allow sunlight to warm the woodland floor throughout late winter and early spring, giving birth to a wonderland of flora and fauna.

Going unnoticed most of the year, as their tender thread-like stems interlace with adjacent sphagnum moss, bluets burst into a mass of sky blue in early spring. Also called Quaker ladies or innocence, they sometimes carpet the smooth stones of creek beds and dangle from moist rocks. Frail and diminutive, they look like small blue fallen stars from the sky.

Beside mountain roads and along fences, small and delicate wildflowers subtly make their unexpected appearances.

A perennial sweet pea is planted by the road department, but escapes into the wild to find a home along sunny roadsides.

The rhododendron is one of the the most popular flowers in the Smokies. They grow in vast thickets called slicks and bloom during midsummer. In the winter, the leaves curl up in a cigar shape to help the plant conserve moisture in freezing temperatures.

Laurel can be confused with rhododendron but an easy way to tell them apart is from the old phrase; short leaf, short name; long leaf, long name.

Confusion exists sometimes because many mountain residents, especially in the past, did not use the term rhododendron. It was often referred to as laurel, while what we usually call laurel was referred to as mountain ivy.

Those who have an opportunity to hike into drifting glades and mountain trails, will find these two flowering plants within the hardwood forests, but beneath them hundreds of wildflowers make their home. The next few pages will give you a small sample of their beauty and variety.

When you find these delicate treasures in the woods the best rule is to enjoy them where they are. Besides being protected by law in the park, most will die if moved to unfamiliar conditions of soil and light.

Yellow Lady's Slipper

Growing in moist, shady areas, the yellow lady's slipper is also known as the moccasin flower because of its unusually shaped petals. They grow twelve to twenty-four inches tall and bloom in April and May.

Trailing Arbutus

The evergreen foliage of the trailing arbutus forms a leafy ground cover as it fans out along paths where there is sandy, acid soil. It is one of the more prized sights to come across. Many wildflower lovers tend to keep the location of these flowers to themselves, even though in some areas they are quite plentiful. The flower is delicately scented and blooms from early March through May.

Bloodroot

Resembling a pond lily and growing about eight inches tall, the flowering season of the bloodroot lasts only a few weeks between March to mid-April. The flower itself only lives a few days and emerges from the hand-like leaves that protect it. If you pick one, the petals will almost immediately fall off. It is a member of the poppy family and gets its name from the crimson-colored juice that comes from the roots. If swallowe it can cause nausea and even nerve poisoning, but early settlers and Indians found it useful to make dye.

Hepatica

The arrival of deeply lobed leaves from the hepatica is a sure sign that spring is on its way. Blooming in March and April, their varying colored flowers range from pure white to pink, and shades of blue and lavender. Usually found in elevations below three thousand feet, the small and tender plants grow only three or four inches in height, with the flower only half an inch across.

Ironweed

The brilliant magenta ironweed grows six to eight feet tall and is one of the showiest flowers of the field. It is most abundant in open and sunny areas of the foothills along roadsides and pastures. Blooms run from late August until late October.

Yellow-Fringed Orchid

There are twenty-nine ↘ varieties of orchids in the Smokies. Open pine forests with their acidic soil and filtered light generally suit them best. Yellow-fringed orchids grow a foot or more tall and flower from July through August.

Joe Pye Weed

Looking somewhat like Ironweed, but less vivid, Joe Pye Weed grows even taller, up to fifteen feet high. Flowering begins in July and continues through September. Although the term "weed" tends to diminish the beauty of these wildflowers for some, they serve to make the Smokies the colorful and varied place it is. They are really no less a weed than any other flower, just more common. Joe Pye was an Indian who used this plant to cure fevers. He traveled to New England with his cure and is one of the very few herb doctors who has had a plant named after him.

Many wildflowers entrust their future to bumblebees. Among them is the thistle, which is rich in nectar. Unlike honey bees, bumblebees are not very social. They build small underground nests of only five hundred to one thousand bees in unexpected places like abandoned mice nests. Their lack of housekeeping is made up for by being extremely hardworking. In fact, bumblebees pollinate more wildflowers than any other insect and the thistle is one of their favorites.

Thistles grow to about thirty inches in lower elevations along roadsides and sunny pastures. Juice from the thistle was once used as a source of medicine for easing the pain of earaches and headaches. The thorny leaves can be quite memorable.

Thistle

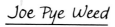

Large-Flowered Trillium

There are ten trilliums in the Smokies. They bloom in the early spring and are members of the lily family. The large-flowered trillium is the most abundant & beautiful. As the flower ages, it turns a rosy pink. Sticky seeds develop and fall from the flower when it dies. Ants love the taste and carry them to their nest. In so doing they actually disperse the seeds for further reproduction. From that point, it can take six years with good conditions for the white trillium to produce its first bloom.

TRILLIUM

Wake Robin →

The wake robin grows along trail sides in the moist woodland floor. It is also called stinking Benjamin because the flower has the unlikely odor of rotting meat. The smell attracts flies, which help with pollination.

Yellow Trillium

Showy Orchis

Appearing in moist wooded areas, the showy orchis blooms on six- to eight-inch stems from April well into May. Colors can vary from white to shades of pink.

Birdsfoot Violet

Thirty-one varieties of violets appear in the Smokies. Unlike most violets that seek moist areas for their home, the birdsfoot violet thrives in dry, open sunny areas along roadsides and trails. It is named for its unique leaf shape.

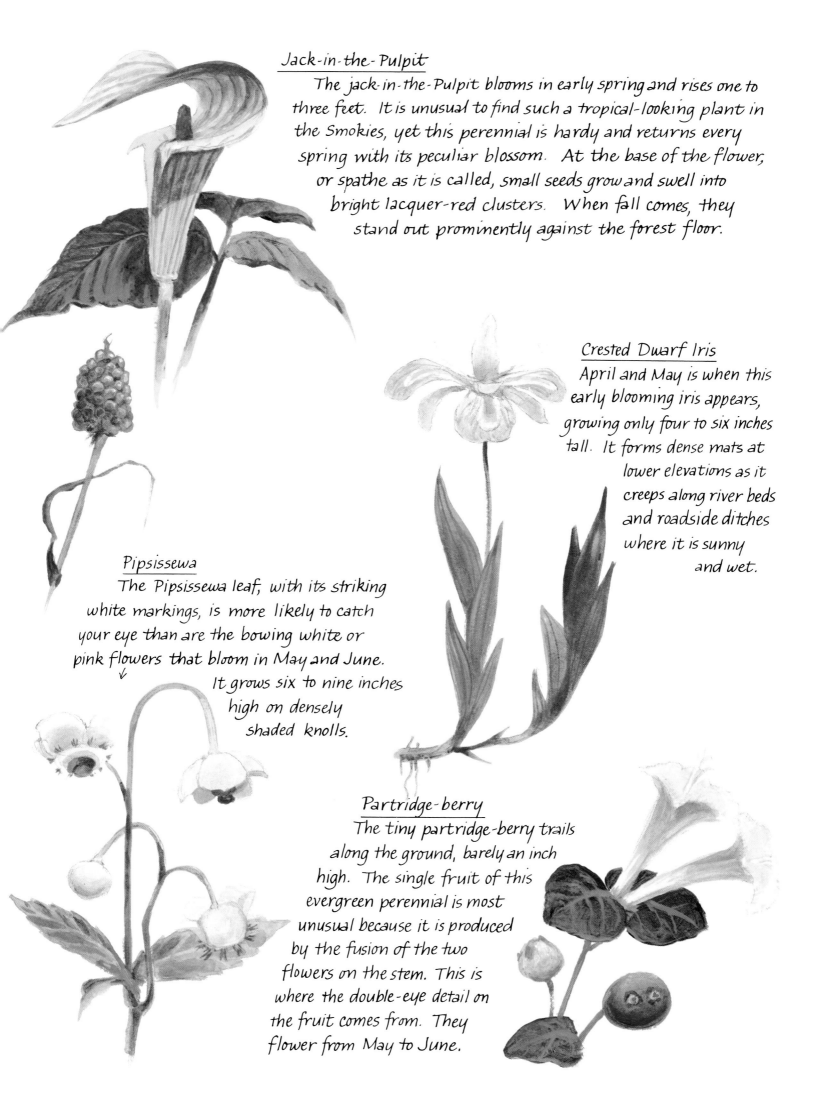

Jack-in-the-Pulpit

The Jack-in-the-Pulpit blooms in early spring and rises one to three feet. It is unusual to find such a tropical-looking plant in the Smokies, yet this perennial is hardy and returns every spring with its peculiar blossom. At the base of the flower, or spathe as it is called, small seeds grow and swell into bright lacquer-red clusters. When fall comes, they stand out prominently against the forest floor.

Crested Dwarf Iris

April and May is when this early blooming iris appears, growing only four to six inches tall. It forms dense mats at lower elevations as it creeps along river beds and roadside ditches where it is sunny and wet.

Pipsissewa

The Pipsissewa leaf, with its striking white markings, is more likely to catch your eye than are the bowing white or pink flowers that bloom in May and June. It grows six to nine inches high on densely shaded knolls.

Partridge-berry

The tiny partridge-berry trails along the ground, barely an inch high. The single fruit of this evergreen perennial is most unusual because it is produced by the fusion of the two flowers on the stem. This is where the double-eye detail on the fruit comes from. They flower from May to June.

Creeping Phlox
Blue and lavender drifts of the creeping phlox bloom in woodland settings of partial shade during the spring. They grow eight to ten inches high.

Wild Sweet William
This taller woodland phlox appears in June along open back-mountain roads. It stands six to eight inches high, and forms colonies of color.

Butterfly Weed →
Butterfly Weed is the most dramatic of all the milkweeds with its blazing clusters of orange flowers. It blooms in midsummer, and the thick, woody tubers can rise three feet or more. This perennial likes sunny locations and sandy soil. Its abundance of nectar makes it a favorite of the butterfly—consequently the name. In the past, the roots were used as a cure for pleurisy and other lung diseases.

Goldenrod
There are eighteen varieties of Goldenrod in the Smokies. They bloom in August and September and grow three feet high. Bees pollinate this plant, and, contrary to what some people believe, it does not cause hay fever, as the pollen is too heavy and sticky to become airborne. The culprit of hay fever is ragweed, which blooms about the same time.

Of all the
wildflowers, a field of
black-eyed susans
appeals to me most.

I'm also
partial to ox-eye daisies
and coreopsis.

It's hard to say what makes a particular scene
attractive to us and why it catches our eye. I have found
the things people like most in a painting, they find least attractive
in real life. Most homeowners would quickly tidy up this situation
of leaves and overgrown shrubs, yet a painting without these leaves
and disarray would not be much of a painting. We love to hang
in a place of honor pictures of the very things we would never
allow in our real life. It's very strange.

There are many different varieties of asters, more than 200 total. Eighteen species are found in the Smokies, but all of them are quite similar. They bloom in the fall after the black-eyed susans have wilted away.

I like to see yards growing freely like this. Wonderful botanical surprises of wildflowers and unusual plants always surface on their own. Too many of the lawns I see are manicured to the point of being very, very boring.

Meadows come alive with color from the many varieties of black-eyed susans and the smaller coreopsis. Summer wouldn't be complete without the sunny faces of these flowers.

If you come across a field of wildflowers
while traveling, don't make the mistake of
ignoring them, thinking that there are more
like it around the next bend.   Altitude
has a lot to do with where they grow,
but not always. Many flowers localize
themselves and are unique to certain
small areas, appearing nowhere else
in the mountains regardless of altitude.
    Poppies are not native to
this area and what you may assume
are wildflowers growing naturally
are actually the result of a
marvelous job of seeding done by
the road department each year.
Such is the case with these poppies.

I can remember picking buttercups when I was a small boy. They would quickly wither away before I could get them home, but even today they remind me of good times and times of wondrous discoveries. It's strange how small things in our lives tend to make large impressions.

The moments we recall from the past are triggered inside us for many reasons. It can be the music from an old song, the smell of burning leaves, or the clear yellow pigment of buttercups growing otherwise unnoticed in an altogether busy world.

Rambling garden roses like these can live for more than a century alongside abandoned houses and cemeteries without any benefit of fertilizers and pesticides. They grow on their own rootstock, unlike most of our modern roses, which are actually two separate varieties joined by grafting. Wild climbing roses only bloom once a year, in June, but when they do they are spectacular.

Why is it that wild roses grow in places that receiv absolutely no care and attention, when at my house I have a hard time getting even one mediocre bloom on a rose bush?

Cades Cove lies on the Tennessee side of the park. New settlers, following Indian trails, started to move here in the 1820's. Soon the trails became roads as schools and churches were built. For 115 years, Cades Cove continued as a working community until it became part of the Great Smoky Mountains National Park in 1934. The population fluctuated, but at its peak there were 685 residents and 132 homes. What remains today is only a sampling of the houses and only a taste of what the lifestyle must have been like.

Rich and fertile soil made farming the main activity in Cades Cove. Beautiful meadows remain, although much of the land that had once been cleared for farming has now been reclaimed by the forests. You can visit this area by taking a narrow but charming eleven-mile loop for a pleasant and rewarding afternoon's journey into the past.

The one thing you don't see much of in the Great Smoky Mountains National Park is a wide expanse of cleared grassland. Cades Cove is one spot where you have a chance to rest your eyes from the usual dense pattern of forest trees.

There are 236 species of birds in the Smokies, ranging from game birds to songbirds. I wish I could paint them all, but here are just a few.

Wild turkeys live on acorns, but also eat insects, grasses and berries. At night they roost together in trees. They can fly up to fifty miles per hour, and can run eighteen miles per hour— they prefer running to flying. Benjamin Franklin fought to make the wild turkey our national bird, but lost out to the bald eagle.

Below a turkey vulture looks for carrion. An unattractive bird close-up, but marvelous to watch as it skillfully rides thermals of air.

Ruby-throated hummingbirds are quite common in the Smokies. They are particularly attracted to red and love hummingbird feeders. A friend of mine uses one and three quarter quarts of water to one cup of sugar, then adds red food coloring. It works quite well.

Their wings create a dull buzzing noise as they beat up to seventy-five times per second. They can fly at speeds of sixty miles per hour.

The camouflage of the ruffed grouse makes him difficult to spot in the woods. It flies only as a last resort, preferring either to run, walk or freeze when threatened.

Along with the cardinal and the
goldfinch, the indigo bunting with
its elegant plumage completes
a trio of primary colors.

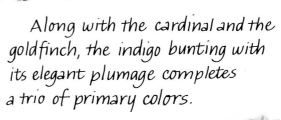

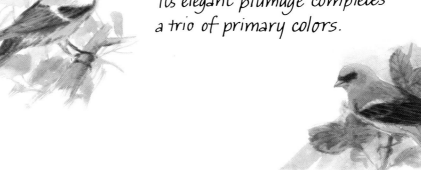

Several paths lead through the woods to John Oliver's cabin,
a first stop on a tour through this once busy but remote settlement,
another path follows the open valley.

The John Oliver house would be a typical 1850's home in this area. An average family was composed of five people, but ten or twelve would not be out of the ordinary.

Coming home to a house like this must have been a luxury for the children after a day at school in Cades Cove. In the late 1800's all eight grades were taught by one person, and the teacher had between eighty and one hundred-twenty students in one room.

Classrooms in the early 1800's had dirt floors with a pit in the center for a fire. A hole in the roof would let smoke out.

The settlers were religious people and their first Methodist Church was established in 1824. A frame church building was constructed in 1902 by the minister. It took him 115 days to build and earned him $115 for the job.

The abandoned nest of the bald-faced hornet can be a real treasure to take home and hang on the mantle. On the other hand, an active nest can result in a painful experience. Paper wasps build these nests from wood that they chew up. A large dwelling can house more than ten thousand hornets.

When there was a death in Cades Cove, a family member or neighbor would go to the church and toll the bell. After a short pause, they would begin again to slowly ring out the age of the person who had just died. By that solemn message, everyone knew who it was.

Weddings were seldom performed at churches. One reason was that drinking was at times a part of the festivities and that was not allowed on church grounds.

This is Cades Cove Missionary Baptist Church, built in 1915. Now it is used only on occasion for special events.

The John P. Cable mill at Cades Cove was built
in 1868 and still runs today grinding corn
for visitors.

Since corn was the primary grain crop, cornmeal would have been the most common
product of a gristmill, although wheat and other grains were also ground at times. Many mills
were operated by farmers and were only open one day a week, usually on Saturday. Young
children would sometimes be sent to the mill perched on the back of a mule or horse with
several bushels of corn to be ground. Most farmers, however, liked to go themselves if time
permitted. It gave them an opportunity to visit with their neighbors.

Some mills had a bell on a post that could be rung to call the miller if anyone needed
grinding done sometime other than the regular grinding day.

Next to the mill is the Gregg-Cable house. It was built in 1897 and later relocated to its present location. As well as being a home, it served as a general store and boarding house.

Even though this was remote, it would be misleading to think that Cades Cove and other areas in the Smokies were isolated from the outside world during this period.

By the late nineteenth century, log houses started to disappear. Frame houses like this one were more prevalent and desirable.

Smokehouses were used to cure meat, although for the most part, the meat was not actually smoked. The curing was achieved by spreading a layer of salt over the meat, sometimes mixed with molasses and other ingredients. Everyone had their own recipe.

The curing process took several months or more and only then was the meat smoked, which furthered the curing and added flavor.

For generations weaving has been a part of the daily routine for the women who helped settle the Smokies. Weavers combined the need for sturdy cloth with their artistic expressions of patterns and color to create fine examples of their skill. It required patience and perseverance.

Of course weaving was only part of the process. Wool had to be sheared from the sheep, washed, dried, carded to straighten the fibers, then spun into yarn on the spinning wheel. Dying was yet another process before weaving actually took place. Once the cloth had been made, it could then be fashioned into clothes, curtains and blankets. Factory-produced thread and cloth as well as clothing were available from many sources, so weaving was usually limited to special items like "coverlets"— what most of us call bedspreads. Families who didn't have much money found weaving more of a necessity.

Here wool is being wound on a ↗ shuttle, which carries the weft back and forth across the warp on the loom.

Whittling a pointed stick can while away a few spare hours on a front porch.

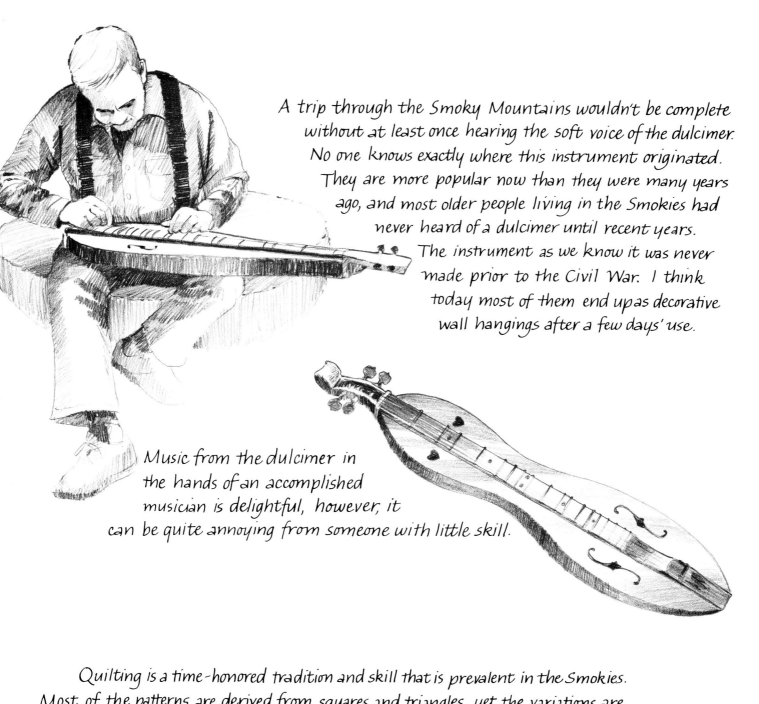

A trip through the Smoky Mountains wouldn't be complete without at least once hearing the soft voice of the dulcimer. No one knows exactly where this instrument originated. They are more popular now than they were many years ago, and most older people living in the Smokies had never heard of a dulcimer until recent years. The instrument as we know it was never made prior to the Civil War. I think today most of them end up as decorative wall hangings after a few days' use.

Music from the dulcimer in the hands of an accomplished musician is delightful, however, it can be quite annoying from someone with little skill.

Quilting is a time-honored tradition and skill that is prevalent in the Smokies. Most of the patterns are derived from squares and triangles, yet the variations are endless. A finely done quilt has between twelve and as many as twenty stitches per inch and can take months or even years to make. Quilting bees, where women gathered to sew on a single quilt, reduced the amount of time it took and afforded the neighbors a chance to visit.

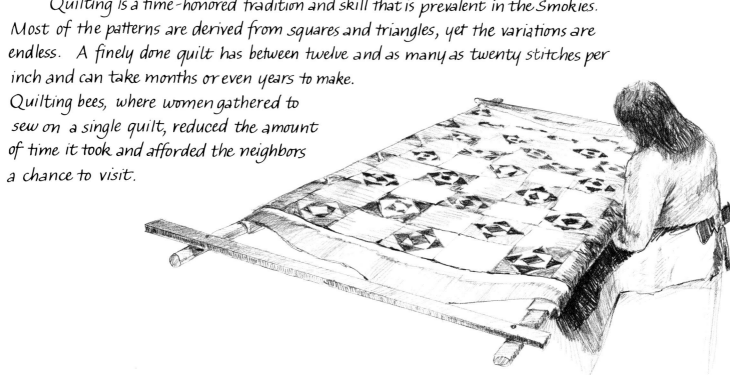

The several barns at Cades Cove accomplish the normal thing barns are made for: housing livestock, storing hay and fodder, and keeping farm equipment from the weather.

This corncrib has two "plunder sheds," as they were called, one at each side.
They were used to shelter extra tools and wagons. ↘

Driving over the crest of a small rise on the back side
of the Cades Cove loop, you will come across this
beautiful weather-worn barn. It has no great
historical significance, but I couldn't resist
stopping to take a look.

My daughters didn't want to pass up the chance to climb in the hay either.
It was the first time they had ever experienced the feel and smell of a real
hay loft. It was as much fun as any ride we had ever been on at any
amusement park, and no waiting in line. Simple things like this often
prove to be the best entertainment. They are adventures that will always
be remembered.

Toward the end of the Cades Cove loop you will pass
the Tipton Place, built in the mid 1800's. Across the road is the barn.
  Small farms would not have much livestock so only a few stalls were needed.
The cantilever barn provided an extra overhang to store harnesses and wagons.
Today, many of the barns you see were once cantilever barns that have been totally enclosed.
The upper part was used to store hay and fodder.

Driving from Cades Cove and all through the Smokies, you will see dogwood blooming as they reach their peak, usually in late April. The flower is actually the small greenish-white center. The white "petals," called bracts, serve as leaf-like coverings that protect the flower before it blooms. As they unfold they turn white.

During the autumn, the leaves turn all shades of red, from a pale pink to a dark maroon. At this time, small red fruit cover the tree – much to the delight of squirrels and birds.

What is now a curiosity was once a symbol of progress that altered the
Smoky Mountains during the early 1900's. The steam engine eventually powered
sawmills and logging equipment and brought the industrial age to the Smokies.
Steam changed not only the landscape, but also the way people lived.
Entire mountains were stripped of trees and ripped
into lengths with the help of steam. Log houses
began to disappear to make way for structures
built from boards.

    Any steam engines that remain today
are used only as an interesting background
for photographs of loved ones.

The soil in the mountains is rich and the rain plentiful, about ninety inches a year in some locations. These agreeable conditions help trees to thrive and make logging to some degree a natural. Today many small mills can be seen along the road. They cater not so much to the industry but to neighbors who want lumber for a new barn, fences and such. Individuals bring the lumber to these mills from their own property for the most part, to be sawed into boards.

Some of the wood milled includes poplar, pine, red oak, white oak, maple, cherry, hickory, ash, spruce and basswood. Chestnut trees, which were once common in the Smokies, began to die in the 1920's and by the late 1930's most were dead or dying because of an introduced fungus from Asia. By the late 1930's every chestnut tree had been killed. Some still sprout up today from old stumps, but they don't live for many years.

This sawmill began operating in the 1950's and now the son carries on the tradition of what his father had started. I did the drawing from an old photograph the son was proud to share with me.

The owner told me that the fifty-two inch blade costs about $2,000 new. A used one would be around $1,000. And if the blade hits an unseen spike driven into a tree, it can abruptly destroy that somewhat hefty instrument.

There are 130 native trees in the Great Smoky Mountains National Park. That is more than in all of Europe, which has only eighty-five. Twenty-five percent of the park is virgin forest and some of the trees reach eight feet in diameter.

I've painted a few of the leaves to help you identify the trees. Here they are:

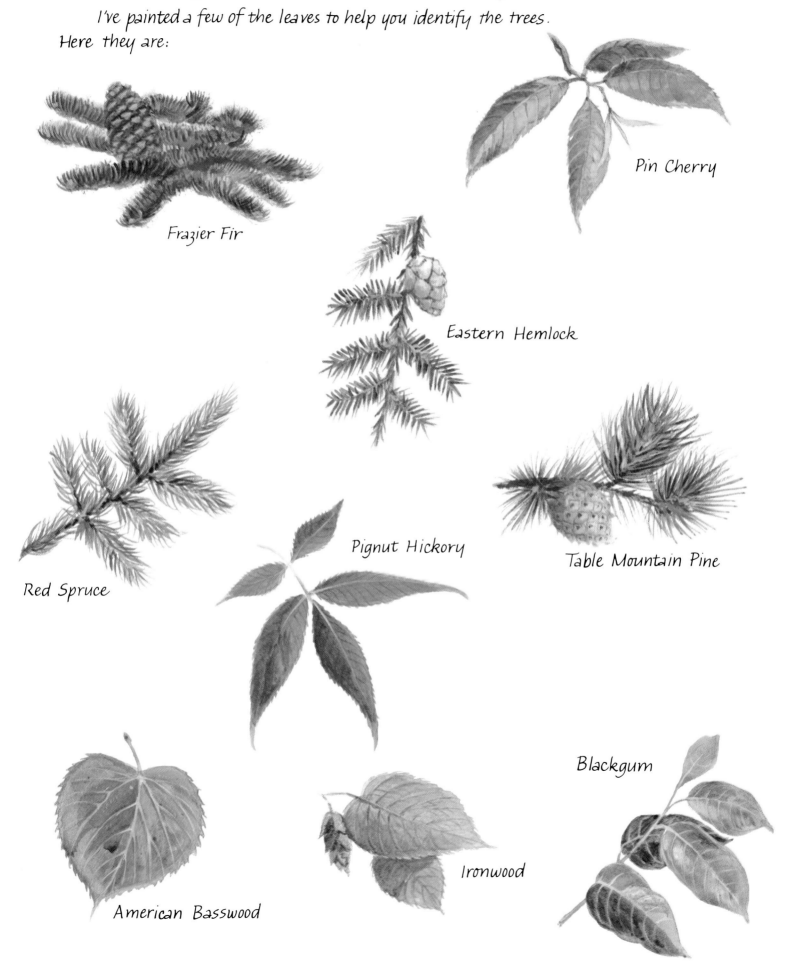

Frazier Fir

Pin Cherry

Eastern Hemlock

Red Spruce

Pignut Hickory

Table Mountain Pine

Blackgum

American Basswood

Ironwood

Mountain Ash

Black Walnut
(brought in)

American Holly

Flowering
Dogwood

Silverbell

Service Berry

Black Locust

Tulip-Poplar

Northern Red Oak

Red Maple

Birch

Sweet Birch

Shagbark Hickory

American Beech

Sassafras

Sourwood

White Oak

Apples are part of a long heritage in the Smokies and they grow well there. Most households would have at least one apple tree in their yard. Businesses grew up around large orchards and today it it is still an active industry.

Apple trees are trimmed at the top to encourage side branching. It also opens up the center to sunlight which increases fruit production. They bloom in April and the fruit is harvested in October.

This packing plant built in 1903, not far from Waynesville, was used to process apples from a 400 acre orchard. Rome, Red delicious, and Golden delicious apples were grown, processed and shipped all over the country. Now, as land has become more valuable and the owners grown older, much of the orchard around the packing plant has been sold to build houses. The plant now stands empty and abandoned.

The thorny blackberry can be found in the summer, growing wild along fences and fields. If you're like me, gathering black-berries for an after-dinner dessert is hopeless, as most of them go directly from the vine into my mouth.

The leaves, when tender, can be mixed with lettuce as part of a salad or boiled like spinach. Dried leaves will make a tea. Be sure to add some honey.

Besides the common blackberry, there are other berries that look similar, such as the southern dewberry, Allegheny blackberry, and the swamp blackberry, which, as the name implies, grows in wet areas. They all look much the same but vary in taste.

When most of us think of the Smoky Mountains, we think
about the Great Smoky Mountains National Park, the Blue Ridge
Parkway, and the "unspoiled" lands that make up those spectacular
eight hundred square miles. Yet as magnificent as the park is, the areas
that have been gently touched by man have a unique loveliness to
them. For the most part, what man has done fits in quite well with
the landscape. The weathered wood of an old barn, the fences,
plowed fields, rusted tractors, all become part of the charm.

Living in the mountain valleys means hard and constant work. Even today, many still grow a substantial portion of their own food. Dealing with nature's elements – winter and the weather, hard clay soil filled with stones, ever-encroaching briars and the constant competition from the wildlife – makes farm work arduous. Deer might be eating the tops of all you've planted while destructive voles are eating all the roots.

In the 1800's, a barn was part of every homestead. No matter whether a husband was a blacksmith or a lawyer, he would still be a farmer to some extent, since every home had a garden. The crops would be used primarily to feed the family and livestock and very little produce would be sold.

The word "barn" originally meant a place for barley, from the old English "ærn" (place) and "bere" (barley).

You don't see it often, but some farmers still plow their fields this way.

This type of roof design is called a gambrel roof, named after the bent part of a horse's leg. It makes good use of interior space.

An old barn, even in disrepair, still adds
some special significance to the landscape.

Here is good hunting for an ambitious cat. What more could a fearless hunter ask for than an abandoned barn where there are lots of mice?

Cats are such independent animals, they rarely care whether you exist or not – except at suppertime - but occasionally they will deliver a trophy to your doorstep just to show you their appreciation of all you mean to them.

I came across these marvelous old contraptions near Asheville.
This machine removed corn from the stalk.

Heavy farm equipment was not found in the mountains as much as in other parts of the country. Work on small farms was mostly done by hand, and owning expensive machines was not practical. Still, crews would sometimes travel from farm to farm with their horse-drawn threshing machines. In the 1930's and '40's farmers in the community would bring their wheat, rye, oats, and corn to the man who owned equipment like this to be processed. It became known as "harvest day" or "thresher day."

This one took the corn off the cob. ↗

Most modest farms wouldn't have had the benefit of a horse-drawn mowing machine to cut hay. It couldn't be used on steep slopes, and for something that was only used occasionally, the investment of even a small machine would be too costly compared to manual labor.

I like the no-nonsense construction of tractors. If only the engine to my car were that accessible. I think the beauty of farm equipment lies in the knowledge that it is functional and not glamorized with unnecessary parts.

Smoky Mountain back roads would not be right without spotting at least a few old pickup trucks being swallowed in the foliage and eaten away with the consumption of rust and time.

What was once a farm tool has now become a nostalgic sales tool.

Early settlers to the Smokies would never have painted their barns. Besides the fact that paint was not readily available, it would have been considered a useless extravagance.

When painted barns later became acceptable, a combination of iron oxide, skim milk, and lime made a red coating that would last many years. If you want to try your hand, here is the receipt.

1½ pounds of oxide of iron
½ gallon of skim milk
8 ounces of lime
4 ounces of linseed oil (use cow's hoof glue, also called mucilage, in case you don't have any linseed oil around the house)

I have owned a balloon for many years and flying in the foothills is always lovely. Cattle generally don't share the enthusiasm of my intrusions.

There is something serene about cattle in the field. Unlike horses, which may conjure up thoughts of adventure and activity, the cow seems to present an absolute statement about contentedly letting the world go by.

Packing loose hay in the field was one alternative to storing it in a barn. Old lumber is placed on the ground first and serves as a bed to keep the hay from soaking up moisture. Then hay is placed around a pole as another person walks on it to pack it down tightly. The tighter it's packed the better. The cone shape, along with raking the hay in a downward position, called dressing, helps shed water. At the very top, hay is twisted and tucked around the pole to help keep rain from running down inside. A well-built haystack can remain fresh for a year or more without rotting.

Today hay is gathered in large rolls looking like giant Shredded Wheat cereal. The theory is the same, tightly packed and baled suitably to shed water.

This old cemetery is on the Little Pigeon River, not far from Gatlinburg. A barn now sits where in 1825 there stood a Methodist Church. Many worshipped here during the Civil War, but the one-room log building was destroyed by a snowstorm in 1886. Another building was constructed that also served as a schoolhouse. It was destroyed by a flood in 1890. Tough times.

The oak tree must have been just a seedling and the headstones recent when all this happened. Now the markers have weathered away along with the names. Wouldn't it be interesting to have known these people? What remarkable stories must be buried here.

The Turk's Cap Lily will brighten up any somber thoughts. They can unexpectedly spring up in sunny areas because their seeds are sown by birds. Once established they bloom year after year in the month of August.

Cigarette smoking has never been attractive to me, however, the labor-intensive process in producing tobacco is quite interesting.

Burley tobacco is the type most typically grown in the Smokies, and for many farmers, it may constitute the main cash crop for the year. It's grown by allotment depending on how much land is owned. If one farmer doesn't want to grow tobacco, his land and allotment can be leased out to a neighbor.

To get tobacco started, the soil is covered with brush and burned to kill weeds and insects. Then it is finely tilled to receive the tobacco seeds, which are left to sprout. They are grown under a canopy of tobacco canvas placed low to the ground to keep the full sun from wilting the plants. In the early spring, when the plants are four to six weeks old, they become large enough to transplant. At this stage they are called "slips".

Here the tobacco is being set in the ground. The tractor makes a hole for the plant and adds some water from that red tank on the back.

Most farmers don't grow enough tobacco to justify a separate barn for drying, so a loft or some part of a general-purpose farm barn is used. A barn constructed specifically for tobacco is usually tall and boxy-looking. Inside, it will contain row after row of racks called "stringers" where the tobacco is hung to cure. During the growing season, farmers must hoe and weed, removing the suckers, and cut the blooms off the tops of the plants as they mature, causing them to fill out. All part of an endless task of maintenance. Some farmers take out hail insurance to protect their investment against a hail storm that can destroy months of work in minutes.

Tobacco grows five to six feet tall. Come late August, it will be cut by hand.
The full stalks of a half dozen plants will be pierced onto a long pointed "tobacco stick."
After a few days curing in the field, all these sticks with tobacco will be taken to the barn.

This wagon is typical of the type used to bring tobacco in from the field.

The tobacco sticks, with their stalks hanging down, are hung between the stringers in the barn, where it cures from a yellow-green to a golden brown. In December it is taken down and "handed off," a term meaning the grading of the leaves. Timing is critical and many factors are involved, such as moisture, color and texture of the leaf. It takes a good eye and experience.

Using a tobacco leaf, the tobacco is tied in small bundles according to grades called "hands" and set in a large shallow basket. Each grade in the basket is then packed on top of each other. From here it goes to the tobacco auction only for the farmer to start the whole process again next year.

I always enjoy seeing the ground hog jutting
its head out from some small hole in the ground.
To a tourist like me, they're an unanticipated visual
pleasure while traveling. Farmers dislike them because
the holes they make in the fields become hazards to the
animals that graze there. Cattle's legs can be easily broken
if they fall into one of the holes while walking along.

They also get into gardens and help themselves to whatever is available. Some people still
eat ground hogs even though the meat is gamey and greasy. Not something that suits my taste.

The hide of the ground hog is very tough, and in days past their skins were sometimes used
for banjo heads. It was also made into shoe laces by cutting long strips in a circular pattern.

The owl is one of those birds that everyone likes. Their image has reached the status of collectible in the form of ceramics and knickknacks at every gift shop. They have become the teddy bear of the bird world.

Owls prey on insects, earthworms, fish, other birds, and, of course, small mammals. Their flight feathers are specialized with soft tattered edges that reduce the vortex noise passing over the wing and make it possible for the owl to swoop silently down on its prey.

↖The great horned owl is among the largest and most powerful.

← The eastern screech owl is small, with "horns" that look much like ears, and add to their likeable character.

⌐ The barn owl needs seventy to eighty acres of hunting territory in order to find enough rodents throughout the year. It is more tolerant of humans than other owls.

Rock City became well-known not as much because of the attraction itself,
but because of the famous "See Rock City" barns. During their heyday, over nine
hundred Rock City barns were painted and repainted regularly, mostly by one man
who could knock out the sign in a day and sometimes do two a day. Now only
a few faded reminders survive.

I guess I'm more nostalgic than I like to admit sometimes. I can remember regularly visiting a little general store much like this when I was a small boy collecting bottle caps from the metal container hung on the side of the soda chest. It was always exciting to discover a brand that I didn't already have. My mom would use some of them too. She would knit around them and make potholders in the shape of a bunch of grapes.

Stores like this are getting quite rare now. Convenience stores owned by indifferent corporations and employing people who never say hello as they sit behind bullet-proof glass have pretty much taken the charm out of it.

Knight's Store has been closed quite a few years now like so many others of that vintage, but merchandise still sat on the shelves last time I looked.

"One man's trash is another man's treasure" certainly stands true when it comes to the "collectibles" that fill roadside antique shops. Popcorn Sutton oversees one such abundant collection of merchandise near Maggie Valley. This admitted moonshiner told me he wasn't making liquor now, but did so for nineteen years and only got caught once. That was back in 1974. His expressive face and long fingers gestured with a shrewdness as he said, "It never stopped me though. I'll make it as long as they sell sugar and water runs downhill." He covered himself by telling me he wasn't making moonshine now, but I presumed by his smile he has some plans about his future.

These are the rural museums of real people and characters like Popcorn Sutton are their curators. Like any museum, it needs security. Mr. Sutton was not shy about posing for me with several of his loaded weapons that he keeps nearby.

I'm sure it takes a herculean effort to find and collect such odds and ends, not to mention all the horse trading that must go on when a purchase is in the works.

It's never given a thought from the casual tourist that stops by, but it represents a lifetime of digging around in forgotten places.

Roaring Fork Road is small and one lane. This isolated and peaceful drive loops from one side of Gatlinburg to the other through a lush mountain forest. The first stop you come to is the Noah "Bud" Ogle farm. The Ogles had the unusual luxury of running water in their house from a nearby spring. It was carried through an open wood trough right into the kitchen where it spilled into a double sink hewn from a large log.

The Ogle family was one of the first to settle in this area. Even today the name Ogle can be seen everywhere you look in Gatlinburg.

Now tightly surrounded by tall forests, this area once had large open fields, and in 1897, it was a busy four-hundred acre farm. On it were apple and plum trees, a garden, hog pens, a corncrib and grazing cattle.

It's a lovely place to walk in the woods with its small streams. Large stumps of chestnut trees killed in the blight of the 1930's still remain in the nearby woods.

Further along on Roaring Fork Road, you will come across this tub mill. Green moss covers the flume and rocks beneath a beautifully tree-covered canopy. At one time there were several hundred tub mills in the Smokies, and nineteen of them were here in the Cherokee Orchard-Roaring Fork Road area. They were one of the factors that permitted the survival of settlements in these isolated areas. It was not only practical to own one's own mill, but it tended to be a statement of social standing as well. This mill was built originally by Alfred Reagan in 1895. Reagan is another very familiar name around the Gatlinburg area. Since the mills were very small and could be hidden away quite easily on mountain streams, some were used successfully to grind meal for blockade liquor.

Tub mills were primarily used to grind corn, and a bushel or so a day was their limit. They were owned and used mainly by one family, but if a neighbor needed grinding done, the use of the mill would have been made available to them for a price. The "toll" as it was called, was usually one gallon per bushel of corn that was ground. Widows or families that were having a hard time were never expected to pay. These mills were always built up on the mountains and when these babbling brooks became flash floods they could be in danger of washing away, as many did.

This drawing shows how they work.

Corn goes in here and gets ground between millstones

Corn comes out here

Floor

Only bottom millstone turns

Rod raises stone to decrease distance between millstones

Flume

Holding Tank

Water turns wheel

Then water spills out

Tub Wheel

The subjects that capture my interest and imagination in the Smoky Mountains are endless. I could paint hundreds more images and not run out of enthusiasm.

Through cool, dense forests with lush vegetation of every description, to high mountains with broad vistas, narrow roads have taken me to many beautiful places. Each view has been like a picture postcard.

These roads led settlers to new lives. Indians traveled them as paths before that. They still twist through mountains and valleys as they did a hundred years ago. In the past, lumber companies with their machinery stripped bare many of these hills, but the forest has returned much as it was. These mountains remain timeless.

The few log homesteads still standing remind us of what life was like. Their scarcity also serves to tell us that what is here now may disappear a hundred years hence. What we do and the things we build are quite temporary.

The people of the Smoky Mountains deserve much credit in leaving things alone as much as they have. Tourists don't think about it, but they come to see and admire what has been left alone, not what has been built up. After absorbing the wonderment of nature and the things time and God have placed here, travelers return to other worlds of concrete and machinery, refreshed and renewed. That is the magic of the Great Smoky Mountains.

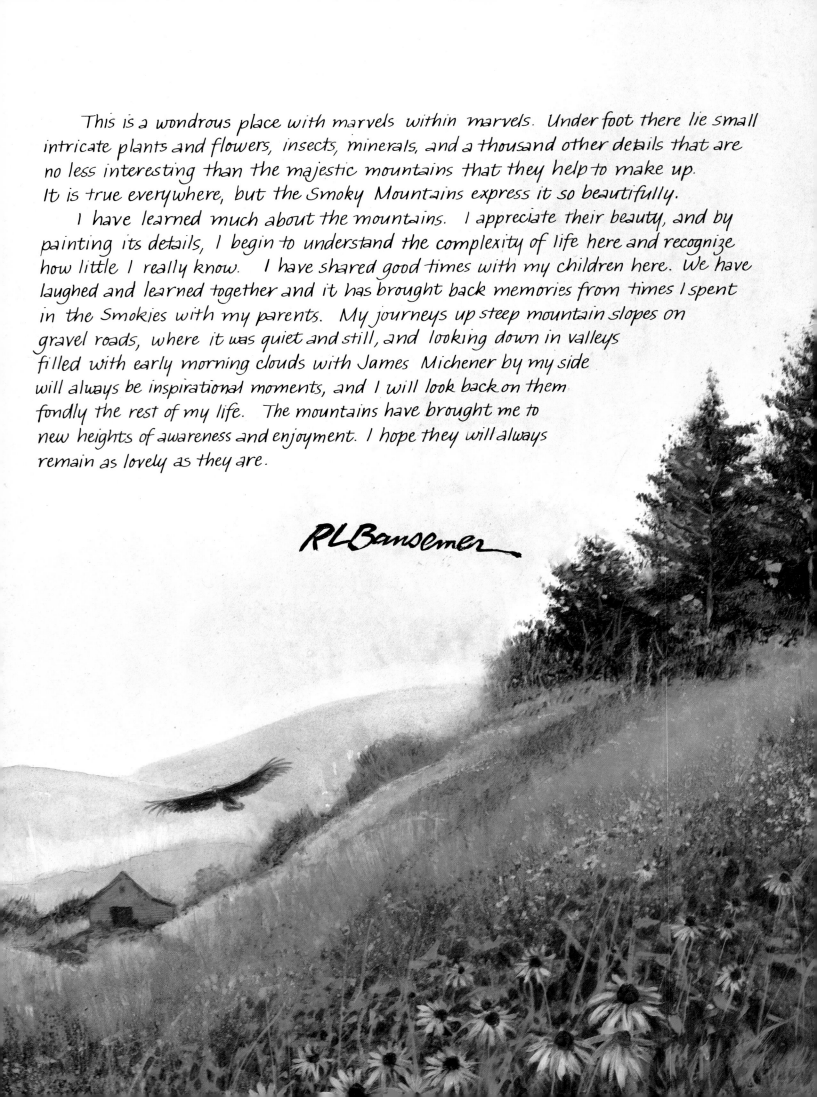

This is a wondrous place with marvels within marvels. Under foot there lie small
intricate plants and flowers, insects, minerals, and a thousand other details that are
no less interesting than the majestic mountains that they help to make up.
It is true everywhere, but the Smoky Mountains express it so beautifully.
    I have learned much about the mountains. I appreciate their beauty, and by
painting its details, I begin to understand the complexity of life here and recognize
how little I really know.   I have shared good times with my children here. We have
laughed and learned together and it has brought back memories from times I spent
in the Smokies with my parents.   My journeys up steep mountain slopes on
gravel roads, where it was quiet and still, and looking down in valleys
filled with early morning clouds with James Michener by my side
will always be inspirational moments, and I will look back on them
fondly the rest of my life.   The mountains have brought me to
new heights of awareness and enjoyment. I hope they will always
remain as lovely as they are.

                        RLBansemer